GET A LIFE

AND

LIVE IT!

Sheilah Gill

Get a Life and Live It
Copyright © 2012 Sheilah Gill

Published by Highly Favored Publishing™
Bowie MD 20716 USA
www.highlyfavoredpublishing.com
Highly Favored Publishing™ is an entity of Highly Favored, L.L.C.

No part of this publication may be reproduced, stored in a retrieval system, or transmitted, in any form, or by any means, electronic, mechanical, photocopying, recording, or otherwise, without the prior consent of the publisher.

The views expressed in this book are solely those of the author and do not reflect the views of Highly Favored Publishing™. The publisher makes no representations about the suitability of the information provided in the material in this book and accepts no liability whatsoever for the validity of the information. The publisher shall not be liable for any commercial or personal damages or loss of profit.

Library of Congress Control Number 1212704111

ISBN 978-0-9835157-7-7

Printed in the United States of America.

This book is dedicated to my parents, the late Dorothy L. Gill, who gave me life, and the late Edward L. Gill, who showed me how to live it!

CONTENTS

Preface	7
The Beginning	9
Childhood	22
The Journey	31
Roadblocks	43
The Destination: Life	51

PREFACE

After 19 years of teaching, I stepped out on faith and took control of my destiny. I took control of the steering wheel, started my engine, and headed down the road of Life. I was sick and tired of life living me! It was time to live life. Because I cared about all students, I refused to turn my back and ignore their needs. However, I was surrounded by many teachers who showed up just to get paid. I felt like a police officer. Parents blamed the teachers; teachers blamed the principal; the principal blamed the school system; and the school system blamed the Board of Education. Because of this, teaching wasn't fun anymore. I was no longer passionate, and I was ready for change!

I became the CEO of my own company, and I began to truly understand the joy of living life. After I left teaching 10 years ago, I was able to never miss a single school program or event my son participated in. I was able to volunteer at his school during the day and donate supplies when needed. Vacations were spent out of the country, sometimes twice a year but always at least once. I took full control of my income, and I have never earned less than $100,000 a year since.

The most valuable thing about living life is the control over my time, the one thing I can never get back. Every day, I am doing what I love, my passion, and I am constantly pursuing my purpose in life! I wrote this book to connect with those who share this passion and to empower those who allow life to live them. I want to teach you the skills necessary to live life and overcome the road blocks that stand in your way.

On this journey, three road maps will follow: red, blue, and green. As you read, select your road map and start your journey with one destination in mind: Life. Each chapter ends with a reflection exercise. Take time to reflect on your personal life by completing each exercise before going on to the next chapter.

Will you join me on the journey of life?

I hope you will,
Sheilah Gill

THE BEGINNING

Most people think life begins the moment you take your first breath, but until you understand the source of life, you merely exist—allowing life to live you. There is a saying, "You can no more give what you've never had than return to where you've never been." This means that until you own your life, until you can stay focused and not allow negative people or circumstances to control your destiny, you cannot give or share it with anyone else. You must know your strengths and weaknesses, love yourself, and constantly work toward pursuing your purpose. These qualities make you whole and allow you to have something to share with someone else. This is beneficial for both personal and business relationships, and this book will give you the necessary tools to live life.

Think back to birth, the moment you first understand you have a life and can communicate your feelings. As a young child, the world is yours, and you will not settle for less. As children, we do not accept "No" easily; we keep trying until we get what we want. We are risk-takers. As children, we must be taught right from wrong. Our guardians are our first teachers, and we are exposed to words like "no," "can't," "stop," and "don't." Our exposure to these terms has everything to do with how we embrace life. As children, we possess a "can-do" attitude that allows us to fall, yet get up. What happens along life's journey that changes our attitude?

This chapter will address three questions:

1. What happens to change people over the years?
2. Why do people stop dreaming and settle for less?
3. Why do we have more dream busters than dream catchers?

The answers to these questions begin with a self-inventory. Are you living life, or is life living you? If you get up every morning and drive to a place you do not like, hang around a bunch of people you wish you did not have to see, and do what you wish you did not have to do, chances are, life is living you! What is even scarier is that you will get up tomorrow and repeat this same pattern again, and again, and again until you get sick and tired of being sick and tired. Get a life! Stop renting your life to someone else, constantly working to fulfill their dream. Find your purpose. Take control. Live life! When you pursue your purpose, you will be passionate about your work, and you will be living life. The question you must ask yourself to help discover your purpose is, "What would I do even if I didn't get paid to do it?"

Over the years, if we allow life to live us, we begin to doubt ourselves. We get caught up in life's challenges and disappointments. We stop dreaming and believing and give in, allowing life to live us. We merely exist, moving day to day with no sense of purpose and no passion about our day. Sometimes, we are in denial and care not to admit it. Think about it, did you run to start your day this morning, or did you dread getting out of bed? Don't worry if you were not thrilled to begin your journey. You can change. *Get a life and live it*!

The great thing about this whole process is that it is never too late to change. However, change is not change until *you* change. Some people allow problems to consume them. They dwell on the problem and allow it to make them miserable, and they create another problem before they can solve the first one. You must embrace life, the good and the bad, and stay focused on your goals. Some things are not in your control. Some things happen as a result of someone else's error, but if you do not live life, it will live you. One of my favorite prayers is by Reinhold Niebuhr. He reflects, "God grant me the serenity to accept the things I cannot change, the courage to change the things I can, and the wisdom to know the difference."[1] Life lessons occur throughout life, and the lessons will repeat themselves until you learn what the lesson is teaching.

For instance, consider Juanita. Juanita met Todd when she was 22. He was everything Juanita thought she wanted. Todd was handsome with a great personality, and he was progressive and full of promises. They dated for four years, and finally, Todd moved in with Juanita. Things seemed to be going very well until Juanita started talk of marriage. With a child coming in April, Juanita felt it was time. Todd shared her views so well that he decided to move out and allow her the space to find a man to marry.

Exactly seven months later, Juanita met Paul, and Paul loved her baby boy. The next year, on Valentine's Day, Juanita was very excited when Paul gave her an engagement ring. Three months later, Paul moved in, and things were wonderful. The only problem was, two years later, Juanita still had no wedding date. Juanita convinced herself it was just a piece of paper, and they did not have to have it. With a second baby on the way, they were too busy to plan a wedding, anyway. Paul felt they should wait because he wanted to save money and finish his master's degree program. Juanita stopped school to work part-time and take care of the kids. It had been four years, and all was well until Juanita started the marriage conversation. Like Todd, Paul loved Juanita too much to stand in the way, so he left. When was Juanita going to learn?

Where you are in your life has everything to do with the people you have allowed to come into your life. You must get control of your life before you can live it. Think about the person in the driver's seat of your life. Who is in control of your future, your destiny? Are you riding in the passenger's seat, or are you in the back seat with no clue of where you are going?

I remember when my son started driving. I was a nervous wreck. I had no control of the wheel, and I found myself screaming, "Stop! Just stop!" I felt I had to get control of the wheel in order to avoid a disaster. Are you driving your car of life? If not, it is time to scream as loud as you can, "Stop!" Prevent a disaster of never living life. Take control!

Find your passion in life and begin to pursue it. Every day we spend so much time making sure other people's needs are met: children, spouse, boss, family members, friends, and others. Until you get passionate about your own life, you cannot do your best for someone else's life.

I remember when I was teaching. I loved it. I was passionate, and it was my purpose. One day, however, it became a job. I was constantly pursuing someone else's passion and controlled by a system I did not believe cared about the children. It was all about the politics. Overnight, I became a paper pusher, test giver, and a glorified babysitter with low income. I shouted, "Stop!" and I resigned. Today, as the CEO of my company, I volunteer in schools and provide free workshops to enhance teachers and students. The lesson here is: Do not rent your life. Put up a "No Vacancy" sign. Let all the naysayers, dream busters, crabs, and pigmy-thinking people in your life know you have no room or tolerance for their dead, dull, disillusioned, whiny, crybaby attitudes.

You have met the naysayers. They are the people who always say no. They are negative and are riding in the back seats of their cars of life, fast asleep. They do not care where they end up in life and settle for just getting by. They live paycheck to paycheck and owe everyone in their lives. This morning, they borrowed bus fare from their twelve year old who earned the money from his paper route.

Remember when you had that conversation about starting your own business. The person you were talking to told you it would not happen. He told you it costs too much and you would never make it. That's right, the dream buster. He sits in the front seat and never wants to drive. He likes riding so he can constantly point out all the reasons why it cannot happen. It is time to pull over and let him out. Tell him to catch a ride because you are not going his way anymore.

Let us not forget about the crabs in our lives. I remember receiving a phone call in 2001. I was given an opportunity for advancement in my business. When I announced my move, there was a lot of support. Everyone was excited. The next day, however, I learned the crabs in my office had plotted to go against me in hopes of getting what I was leaving behind. They convinced many to stay behind, hoping I would not be successful. They never saw the blessings to come. The old company was producing $350,000 a year. My new company produced over $1.4 million. They still have no idea what they could have been a part of. In life, crabs will grab onto you and pull you down to their level.

Fight like a crab in a bucket to get out. Shake them off.

Lastly, we meet the pigmies. They are tiny-thinking people who cannot see over the dashboard. People with this mentality do not even know where the car is. They can be found in the parking lot waiting for someone to leave their keys in the ignition. When you talk about pursuing your goals, thinking out of the box, or making a six-figure income, they laugh. They think you are crazy because in their world, a little is a lot. They will never drive the car because they cannot reach the steering wheel. Let them ride; they are really no bother to you. They are irritating, but sometimes fun. You will look up one day, and they will be gone. Or, they will ride with you long enough and change.

The hardest part of living life is first getting one. To get a life you must start by finding yourself. Where are you, and where do you want to go? This book will make you look yourself in the eye. It will strip you naked and force you to look. Frightening, but do not worry. You might not like what you see, but change is going to come.

Perhaps, you are not ready for change. If not, you are closing the book now. If you decide to close the book, be sure to place it somewhere for safe keeping. You can read it now or read it later, but trust me, at some point in your life, you will be ready to read it. You have to reach a point in your life when you are tired of life living you, and you have to make a decision to live life!

The decision is the biggest step. People will do more to avoid pain than they will do to get pleasure. That is why until it hurts badly enough, you will never change. That reminds me of a story I once heard. Allow me to share it with you:

> One day, a man was walking down the street on his way to work. As he walked down the street, there were dogs on just about every front porch, and they all would bark as the man passed them. However, there was one dog he remembered because this dog was just sitting there, and he was whimpering and whining and moaning. You know the little whimpering sounds dogs make when they are wounded or in some sort of pain. Well, this particular dog was just sitting there on the front porch making those sounds. The man was curious as to why this dog wasn't barking like the other dogs and why he was whimpering. He couldn't figure it out, so he just kept walking to work. The next day, he was in the same situation where he was walking down the street and saw the dogs, and this same dog that was moaning and groaning the other day was doing the same thing that day. He just couldn't figure it out. Well, he walked past for an entire week, and every day the dog would be there moaning and groaning. Finally, the guy got fed up. He said, 'Let me find out what's going on.' So he went and knocked on the door, and a guy came out and said, 'Yes, how may I help you?' He said, 'Sir, is

this your dog?' 'Yes, that's my dog.' 'Well, what's wrong with him?' The owner of the dog said, 'What do you mean?' 'Well, he's been sitting here moaning and groaning, whimpering and whining for an entire week. The rest of the dogs are barking. Your dog should be barking, too. Why is he moaning and groaning?' The owner said, 'Well, he's actually sitting on a nail.' He said, 'What! Your dog is sitting on a nail. Why doesn't he get off?' 'Well, it just doesn't hurt him enough.'[2]

Have you ever wondered why someone would stay in an abusive relationship, or in any relationship, where they were not happy? People have their own levels of tolerance. As you read this book, if you are not sick and tired of being sick and tired, my goal is to help you reach your breaking point. There is so much waiting for you when you begin to live life. Peace, happiness, and love, just to name a few. Living life is the most rewarding thing to do.

Let's start in pursuit of ownership. Tap into your Source. God don't make no junk! There is no fear. Self-esteem either has been given to you, or it has been taken away. If it was taken, you must demand it back! Remember, you are driving and you decide your direction. There will be few rest stops, and when we do stop, we will not stop long. We have no time to waste. Fasten your seat belt, adjust your mirrors, and let's start toward our destination: Life!

REFLECTION ONE: THE BEGINNING

1. What is your passion? What would you do for free because you enjoy it that much?

   _____
   _____
   _____

2. If you were starting your own business, what would you do? What do friends and family always admire about you?

   _____
   _____
   _____

3. Who are the five most influential people in your life?

   _____
   _____
   _____

4. Of the five people you mentioned in number three, who is where you want to be?

   _____
   _____

Identify each person in question 3 using one of these titles: Naysayer, Dream Buster, Pigmie, Crab, or none of the above.

PERSON   **TITLE**

1. _____   _____

2. _____   _____

3. _____   _____

4. _____   _____

5. _____   _____

Let's put this car in park and determine just how long this journey to Life is going to take.

There are three road maps, and you must decide which map is yours. If you choose the wrong road map, your journey may be longer and harder than you ever imagined. Read carefully and be true to your choice.

The Red Map

This map is found with the individual who grew up with a bad childhood. There was very little love, if any, and the lessons learned were more street lessons than book lessons. By the time you were a teenager, if not before, you carried the responsibilities of an adult. Life was hard, and you were angry. Teachers could not reach you, and most people in your life had stopped trying. Remember your first serious relationship? What a joke. There was so much arguing and fighting that it just became the way of life. Now, you cause havoc everywhere you go. You are so focused on your failures that you resent other people's success. Successful people are a clear picture of who you know you want to be. Understand that you will be a success if you just let go of the pain. Put your negative energy into positive success.

There is more to life than merely existing. Stop and shout, "By whatever means necessary! Enough is enough!" "Who cares?" you must ask. Remember, God don't make no junk, and regardless of what some irresponsible individual may have passed on to you, it is time to take back your keys and drive your own car. From this day forward, you must take back your life and not allow them to control your destiny any longer. You are the driver.

The mountains are extremely high, and the valleys are extremely low. Watch out for that river of unending tears. Self-esteem has become a road block, and you can't see the forest for the trees. But guess what, the route can be changed. Throw away your red map, turn off your OnStar, and follow these directions: Start down *I am Somebody Lane*, and turn right onto *I Can Do All Things With Christ Who Strengthens Me Lane*. Go past three *You Can't Do It* stop signs, and turn left onto *Positive People Drive*. You will see a gas station on your left where you can pick up a new map. Your destiny is Life, and there is only one person who can put you on the right course. Tap into your Source. If you decide today to tap into your Creator, you will never be lost again. You may be a victim, but you do not have to stay a victim. I know your road is rougher than most, but I also know you can make it. Take your time and read this book. Do not settle for door #1. If you will take a chance, the next door will be much more rewarding.

The Blue Map

This map is found with the driver who is hurting or in pain. Perhaps you grew up in a single-parent home and have resented the absence of the other parent. This person may have lost a parent through death or divorce. This person may have experienced a bad relationship. Circumstances happen, and sometimes, we have no control over the hand we are dealt. What is important is how we choose to play the hand. No one can dictate your life's journey. They can mentor, motivate, and guide, but at some point, you have to grab the wheel and drive. Storms are okay if you focus on how to weather them and not how long you will stay in them. Life's journey brings many people into our lives, and every relationship has a purpose. Sometimes, we get caught up focusing on the bad in a relationship. Relationships are beautiful, and you always know when they begin. However, you never know when they will end. Learn to take the good and walk away from the bad. Grow from the experience, but do not dwell on it. Recognize when it is over, and keep it moving.

Many people take love for granted. When you are taken for granted, it hurts. Each relationship takes something from you. I heard this best explained once using the analogy of a pie. You have a lot of pie slices to give away, and your first love gets a big piece. Each relationship takes a slice out of your pie, and you get to a point where you have one sliver left. You hold on to this last chance for love, and you are very cautious of whom you give it to because it is your last chance. But, it is not your last; just bake another pie!

Every person you meet has to compete with all the pain and disappointment you have experienced with bad relationships. Please, turn your windshield wipers on. Boo, hoo, hoo, your windshield is full of rain from your tears. You cannot trust, and you are always expecting the worse from a relationship. No matter what your partner does, you always find the negative in it. You want to travel forward, but there is no room for your suitcase because the trunk is full of all the baggage you carry every day. Release, relax, and run from your past.

Get a life! Let go of the baggage. You cannot move forward if you are stuck in the past. Start your vehicle of life. Go forward in faith. Turn left onto *Happiness Lane*. Go past Heartbreak Hotel. You will see a gas station on your left where you can pick up a new map. Your destiny is to live life and not allow life to live you. Learn to love yourself, and you never will have to depend on someone to do it for you. Do not allow past relationships to dictate future ones.

The Green Map

This map is found with people who remain positive and happy through all the storms of life. They let nothing hold them back. What would make this person welcome storms in their life? They have strong family roots, and their values will not be compromised. When you realize that after every storm there is a rainbow, you can begin to focus on what happens after the storm — which allows you to move through the storm as fast as possible.

I am reminded of Sean. Sean had a loving family. He and Dana had their share of problems, but Sean had his own successful business. Dana traveled because of her retail sales manager position. The kids were happy and all seemed fine. Years went by, and Dana began to consume herself with activities outside of the house. Sean was at all the school PTA meetings and attended all the kids' outside activities. It was no surprise when Dana asked for a divorce, but even though Sean knew it was coming, reality did not set in until the divorce papers came. Sean consumed himself with "Why?" Was she in love with someone else, was she homosexual, or had she lost her mind?

Sean's business began to suffer, and he lost focus of everything important. Dana moved on, remarried, and never looked back. Sean needed to let go and let God.

It is hard to move past a broken heart. You wonder, "What happened to love?" If a person finds happiness somewhere else, should they remain where they are not happy? This is one of the reasons why people cheat. If people would get a life and then share it, there would be fewer divorces. People marry for the wrong reasons. Then, they discover their lives but find their partners are not the people they want to live their lives with! I guess Tina Turner said it best when she said, "What's love got to do with it?" Too many people lose everything during the storm because they do little or nothing to get through it. They give up, settle for less, and bury their dreams. Childhood experiences lay the foundation for our futures. We must understand who we are and where we came from. Then, we can make a decision to change where needed. If we do not deal with our past, we stay stuck in the past. We grow in size and age, but we never grow in life. It is time to put your car in drive, press the gas, and head toward Life!

REFLECTION TWO: CHILDHOOD

1. Which map best describes your past?

   _____

2. How has your past affected your future?

   _____
   _____
   _____

3. Name a person from your past who has had a major influence on where you are today?

   _____

4. Was this person's influence negative or positive?

   _____

If negative, what can you do, or what have you done, to prevent this person from influencing you further? If positive, what can you do, or what have you done, to maintain this influence?

Negative:

_____
_____
_____

Positive:

_____
_____
_____

THE JOURNEY

Before we depart, there are three things I need to make sure you have: attitude, belief and commitment. I call these the ABC's of life. Your **attitude** is everything. This journey begins with you and the decisions you make. Your attitude is what compels you to crawl, walk, or even run to your destination. It does not matter which method you take as long as you get there. In life, everyone will not run at the same time. Your attitude will allow you to embrace those who go before you. Some people do not want to see another person go first. That is jealousy. Many times, people are afraid because they know they are losing a person from the "do nothing club." Sometimes, people are so caught up in other people's success they never reach for their own. To grow, you may have to let go. It is hard to leave people you care about behind, but if you do not go first, they may never get there. Remember, you can always come back and get them. You have to see it to seize it. Attitude is the "want to." You must *want to* pursue your purpose and your goals, and you must refuse to let anyone or anything get in your way.

Now that you *want to*, you have to **believe** that you can. I think faith is the deciding factor that determines whether you crawl, walk, or run toward your goals. It may be easier for individuals who had people in their lives who told them they could be anything they wanted to be. They had support and were encouraged to never give up. This is why it is so important to have a mentor and, more importantly, become a mentor to a young person. When you reach your destination, Life, you will be ready to become a mentor. Decide who your mentor is and get around that person every chance you get. Watch and study the person through books, music, or in person. By whatever means necessary, connect with your mentor. Belief enhances your self-esteem, and having positive people to support you helps you believe you can make it.

Here is where we ride past the ocean. It's okay to be afraid to tread new waters, but understand you cannot see the ocean until you lose sight of the shore. In order to progress, you cannot stay where you are. Moving forward allows more opportunities. You must be **committed** to staying the course until you get where you are going. People who quit usually quit one day too soon. Nothing worth having comes easily. This is where your faith and perseverance will be tested. No matter how rough the road is, keep going.

After you have mastered the ABC's of life—your attitude is right, you believe in yourself, and you are committed—you are ready to begin your journey.

Prior to this journey, you may have had many coaches in your life. Now, it is time to make sure your coaches truly care about your success. I remember a football coach my son had in high school. The team fought hard and took much pride in working as a team. Through every loss, their spirit brought them back on the field to fight again. Due to a losing season, however, a new coach was selected. He was selected based on how many championship games he had won. Surprisingly, with all his fame and glory, the team lost again, and they also lost their pride and their team spirit. The new coach cared nothing about the players; it was all about his reputation. The best coach is a coach who cares about you. Everyone needs a good coach, a support system. The books you read, what you listen to, and the people you hang around are your immediate coaches. They will be the support you need as you complete your journey. Park your car, gather your equipment, and let's start on our first journey toward Life.

Our first journey takes us up a mountain. When faced with a mountain, you must climb it. If you are not ready for the climb, you must find a way to go around it or find a way to go through it. All of our lives we have been faced with mountains. Once you reach the top, you can appreciate the climb, and you will know you did it and can do it again. If you go around the mountain, you will not reach your full potential. If you go through the mountain, you are following a path that has already been paved, and it may or may not be the path to your success. As children, we climb for approval. The question is, "As a child, whose approval were you after?"

What happened in your childhood has a direct impact on your future. Everyone must learn to recognize a positive versus a negative impact. At a birthday party, people celebrate a new year. People need to learn to celebrate change. This is a time to continue the road we trod or to take a turn in a new direction. Even if you suffered through poverty, alcoholism, drug abuse, physical abuse, mental abuse, or were forced to raise yourself without guidance at an early age, you can still thrive. What matters is how fast you will make the decision to move forward in spite of these negative experiences. Some people go through life thinking, "What if …?" They never let go. One person's opinion does not have to be yours. Have you ever spent more than five hours in a workplace where you did not believe in anything they stood for, and if they took away the paycheck you would quit? Why did you stay? Change is not change until you change!

As a child, I watched a game show called "Let's Make a Deal." The host would pick someone from the audience and have them select door number 1, door number 2, or door number 3. People would select one door, and when given the opportunity to trade for another door, they would say no because perhaps they had already won a new living room and floor-size color TV. They settled, and when the door they turned down was revealed, they found they had turned down an all-expense paid trip around the world with cash to spend. Most people will settle for what is comfortable. Change is uncomfortable, but when you get to the other side of change, it is always beautiful. Think about the caterpillar that changes into a beautiful butterfly. It starts as an egg, becomes a caterpillar, stops eating, and wanders to find a place to pupate. Later, it turns around and retraces its path, releases its hold, drops downward, and pupation begins as it emerges into a beautiful butterfly, ready to spread its wings and fly.

As children, we climb for approval. As young adults, we climb for position. As adults, we climb for success. This book is intended to help you start your climb and never stop until you reach the top.

ARE YOU READY TO CLIMB?

Every action has a reaction. Instead of spending a lot of time focusing on the problem, you want to focus on the solution to the problem. Some people stay in a relationship long after it is over. They are focused on the break up instead of what they will do after the break up. Others break up on Monday and are in a new relationship on Tuesday. Their partner is stunned. How can this be? While they are hosting a pity party, their ex-partner is progressively moving forward. I know this sounds cruel, but life is cruel. That is why you have to learn to live it, or it will live you!

I truly believe men leave a relationship long before women. Most women struggle, even after a relationship ends, trying to figure out what happened. If they really think back, there were signs long before the men left. Men know where they are going before they leave from where they are. That is why they have problems asking for directions. It seems very simple, but women put up with and hold on longer than men. If you are thinking you are the exception, then so be it. Just be sure you are not in denial. Denial is a major road block on your journey. It is worse than a setback. When you have a setback, you know you need to regroup and move forward. Denial keeps you where you are, and you have no clue you need to move forward.

This journey is hard. Climbing any mountain is hard. You have to have the right equipment and the right mentality to deal with the climb. Every individual has her or his own mountain to climb. It is usually around age 25 that you can identify your mountain, although there is no set age because individuals are unique and everyone's circumstances are different. Some people do not start their climb until late in life. This is because they are so busy holding someone else's hand it delays their climb. They spend too much time talking about how well someone else is climbing and are not focused on their climb, or they are in denial and do not realize they even need to climb.

There will be many obstacles during your journey. Do not focus on the problem. Stay focused on the solution. After every storm, there is a rainbow. Your solution to every obstacle is to decide how long you will dwell on the problem versus how quickly you will move toward the solution. You have no control over when the problem comes, but you do control how long it will last. I attended one of Les Brown's motivational conferences in Washington, DC a few years ago, and something he said stuck with me. He said, "If you fall on your face, roll over because if you can look up, you can get up!" No one wants to hear your problems, and you certainly do not need to hear them again. Do not host a pity party. This may seem cold and uncaring, but this is life. You live it, or it will live you. Society tells us go to college, get a job, get married, have kids, buy a house, get in debt, and teach your kids to do the same. Escape so you can begin your journey.

I teach seminars on starting your own business, and the hardest thing an adult has to learn is how to dream again. Learn to look for the positive in every situation. Here's a story to consider. There were two little boys, and one was always negative and the other always positive. An experiment was performed to see if their attitudes would change. The negative boy was put in a room with all his favorite toys, anything a child his age would desire. The positive boy was placed in a room full of horse manure. After an hour, they returned to the negative little boy to find him sitting in the middle of the room crying. Astounded, they asked what could possibly be wrong. You have everything. He whined that all the toys were broken, and he wanted to go home! In the next room, they found the positive boy jumping up and down shouting, "Wow!" Horse manure was everywhere. They asked, "What are you doing, child?" He replied, "With all this manure, there must be a pony in here somewhere!" It does not matter the circumstance, like the positive boy in the story, you must decide to always find the positive! Life is what you make it, not what it makes of you. Get a life!

As you proceed on this journey, understand that your lifestyle, relationships, and career choices may go through some changes. However, you must accept change and welcome happiness and fulfillment. You may find that you have spent years wasting precious time, but time is one thing you can never get back. Be steadfast along this journey. You do not want to waste any more time. I watched a movie one time called *The Bucket List*. It was about two male strangers who met each other in a hospital room where they found out they both were dying. They decided to pursue completing a list of all the things they ever wanted to achieve. They found themselves laughing and enjoying life to its fullest.

Do not wait to find out you are dying to begin living life. Do it now!

My son was in high school when he said to me, "Dream as if you'll live forever and live as if you'll die today!" Why do we stop dreaming? Some people see the negative in every situation. They are so blind they cannot find the positive.

There is a story of a boy who walked along the beach, and the late evening current kept washing starfish to the shore. The little boy picked up one after the other and threw them as far as he could. A man pointed out the current would never allow him to save them all. He told the boy that what he was doing didn't matter. As the boy threw one as far as he could, he turned and replied, "To that one it does!"[3] We cannot save the world, but we can certainly save ourselves. Go for it one more time. Stretch your vision . . . dream!

REFLECTION THREE: THE JOURNEY

Develop your Bucket List now. Make a list of at least 10 things you want to do before you leave this earth.

1. _____
   _____

2. _____
   _____

3. _____
   _____

4. _____
   _____

5. _____
   _____

6. _____
   _____

GET A LIFE

7. _____

8. _____

9. _____

10. _____

After climbing the mountain, we return to our car and continue our journey. Watch out for the road blocks. Finding out who you are is so important at this point. You cannot go further in your search for life until you know who *you* are. If your picture were in the encyclopedia, what would be the description next to it? Who are you? How do the people closest to you describe you? There are so many people stuck at a road block because they have failed to discover who they are. If you can admit your faults, you can begin to correct them.

A key to knowing yourself is liking yourself and not caring what others think about you. When you like yourself, you are positive in your thinking. You are concerned with helping others. You are a thermostat in the room and not a thermometer. You set the temperature; you do not wait for the room to warm. You realize the show cannot be all about you, so you have no problem recognizing greatness in others.

If the above paragraph does not describe you, do not worry. It just reinforces that we have work to do. If it does describe you, still continue reading so you will know how to identify and help others who need to discover who they are.

People in search of themselves are usually people with low self-esteem, but you must understand that low self-esteem is not self-inflicted. It could be from a past environment or a current environment. It could be due to a past relationship or a current relationship. Regardless, you need to identify where it came from so you can move forward.

I once had a good friend whose religious beliefs taught we choose our parents. I can only say that if I had a choice, I would have chosen the same parents I had because it was wonderful to grow up in a loving environment with two parents constantly working for the enhancement of our family. However, I understand this ideal family life is not every person's reality. I have a good friend who would say if he had a choice, he never would have chosen the parents he has.

Regardless, honor thy parents and your days will be longer is what the Bible says. It does not say honor them if you think they were good parents. They did the best they knew how to do. They may have been an example of individuals who never changed. Maybe they let life live them. Perhaps they allowed negative parents to dictate who they became, and they never accepted their pasts and moved forward. You cannot get stuck. You must decide to move forward. We know parents can be a positive or negative influence. Regardless, each of us has a choice to endure and duplicate our parents' past or to escape it.

Recently, a very successful and famous person shared that his father walked out of his life when he was 13. It was not until his father died, when he was 32, that he let go of the pain the abandonment had caused. He further shared that he was unsuccessful in relationships because he never wanted to let another person get that close to him. Imagine holding on to the effects of a past relationship for 19 years. Do you know how many people live life like this? They are victims, and they stay victims until they accept the problem and move toward the solution.

It is so easy to play the blame game. Sometimes the solution is right in our faces, but because we do not have to apply any effort, so long as it is someone else's fault, we focus on the problem and point the finger. However, when you point your finger at someone else, there are three pointing back at you.

It's like the joke about the man who has been notified that a storm is coming and his house may be flooded. He is told to get out of the house. He says, "No, I don't have to. God is going to take care of me." Then the flood starts to rise, and a sheriff comes along and tells him to get out. The man says, "No, God is going to save me." So, the floods continue to rise up to his second floor window, and a boat comes along. He's told to climb into the boat. He says, "No, no, God is going to save me." Quickly, the water rises more, and he finds himself on the roof of the house. Finally, a helicopter comes along, and they lower the net to rescue him. The man says, "No, no, God is going to save me!" Well, the man drowns and goes to heaven. When he gets to heaven, he says to God, "Why didn't you save me?" God says, "I sent the sheriff. I sent a boat. I sent a helicopter. What more did you want me to do?"[4] I reference this story because a person either chooses to accept the hand he has been dealt or to change the cards. I love to play Scrabble, and one rule in the game is if you do not like your letters, you can throw them in and get new ones. Play Scrabble with your life. If you do not like it, throw it in for a new one. Your past does not have to dictate your future. One screwed up individual does not have to screw up your life up. You cannot reach your potential carrying the burdens of past relationships.

As long as you carry baggage, you allow someone else to win. Your journey begins with the acceptance of your burdens brought on by past circumstances and the willingness to do whatever it takes to drop those burdens like a bad habit and change. Take control by putting your foot down and saying, "No more." It will not be easy to change. It took years to get where you are, and it will take time to change. It may even be more than you can do alone. You may need a mentor or even counseling. However, until you deal with your burdens, they will delay your journey. How long have they already set you back, and how much longer will you allow them to continue to delay your journey to Life?

Change needs to happen because *you* want it, not for someone else. Most people who make changes to please someone else do not continue the change. If they change for themselves, they are more likely to maintain the change. I have had girlfriends who meet a new man and lose weight, dress differently, and wear their hair differently. As soon as the new man leaves, they gain the weight back and go back to their old clothes and old hairstyles. When you make changes for yourself, they are lasting changes. How long it takes to change will determine how long your journey to Life will be. You cannot make changes until you accept that the past is the past. You cannot allow the past to determine your future. Let go and let God!

Every individual has to travel down his own road. Some roads will have more twists, turns, bumps, and hills than others. It really does not matter how long the journey, as long as you stay focused on your destination . . . Life! When you get a life, then you can start to live it!

REFLECTION FOUR: ROAD BLOCKS

In each bag, list five things you have carried long enough. *Release* this baggage, *relax* by letting go, and *run* in the opposite direction.

In your family life, what baggage can you leave behind?

1. _____
2. _____
3. _____
4. _____
5. _____
5. _____

In your relationships, past and present, what baggage can you leave behind?

1. _____
2. _____
3. _____
4. _____
5. _____

List any other baggage you will leave behind starting now!

1. _____
2. _____
3. _____
4. _____
5. _____

When you take power back from anything and anyone in your past that has prolonged your journey, you will bring peace and happiness to your life. I recall a 45-year-old male who admitted he finally realized why he was single. The hurt and pain caused by his first and second relationships had made him afraid to ever let anyone get that close again. He realized this after losing the one woman he really loved. He pushed her into the arms of someone else by keeping her at a distance. It is amazing how we will do more to prevent pain than we will do to receive pleasure.

Once you get your life back, you can begin to *live* life. Until you get to the end of finding life's journey, you will not have a life. You will rent it out to anyone willing to sign a lease. However, when you get to your destination, your goals will get accomplished. You will begin to dream again, and you will find yourself loving life. You will find that your friends may be different because you will not have a lot of tolerance for people who try to take you off your path. Everyone around you will bring happiness, and if they do not, you will not be around them long. You will be there to encourage them and to mentor them through their journey. However, you will not allow them to get in the way of reaching your goals.

Life gives us what we demand from it. You must decide what you want from life. So many people settle and just get by. They work all their lives, retire, and die. What will your eulogy say? How many people will come to hear it? This might sound morbid, but this is a direct reflection of how you lived your life. I recently attended a funeral. The entire service exemplified the great person we were there to mourn. I think the most comforting moment was at the repast. I sat at a table where the only person I knew was the person I came with. I listened as one person after the other shared stories of the things the deceased person had done to touch their lives. They spoke of what a joy and honor it was to have known her. I knew she was a remarkable person, but I had no idea how many lives she had touched. It was comforting to know she was tired and the Lord had brought her home to rest. We were blessed to have known her. One morning, she sat down to breakfast and went home to her Lord. No pain and no suffering. She had lived life!

As a former school teacher, it concerns me what we teach our children. So many leave their children burdened. So many people lie dormant, never releasing their potential. They are robbing the next generation of their talents. Ask yourself, "What am I passing on?" After age 40, your legacy should be a major concern. So many people are underinsured or not insured. If you die in debt, your children will inherit debt. Sure, they can walk away from all that you have accomplished, but that is very hard to do. I remember when I quit my JOB, you know, my Journey of the Broke. I know everyone will not be an entrepreneur, but if you must work a job, love what you do or leave as soon as you can to run to what makes you happy. I worked part time as an entrepreneur until I was able to quit my job and run my own company as the CEO. Get a life and fix it. If it is not broken, then leave it as it is. Some of us became financially responsible a long time ago, and I hope those who have not will start today.

A major factor in reaching your destination, Life, is financial responsibility. When you reach your destination, your money has to be in control. You must earn it and not burn it. Reach out to others less fortunate and make a difference in your community, but remember, charity starts at home. Throughout life's journey, you must pay yourself first. The longer you wait to apply this principle, the longer it will take to reach your destination . . . Life!

People who never gain control of their finances are limiting their love of life because they are always playing catch up. They cannot expand their vision because they are stuck with limitations. Money is not everything, but it can help you find everything you need to live life.

When you tap into your Source, my Source is God, you can arrive at your destination. He can be your Source, too. He will always be there to help you reach every goal you set. He is waiting for you to make a move. One step forward is all it takes. We have ministering angels waiting to help us reach our potential. They want us to live life abundantly. The problem is they are sitting in a room playing cards, bored, because many do not summon them for help.

At this point, if you have completed all the reflections, you are ready to live life. If not, read the book again. This book was written for you. It might take more than one reading to implement these principles. How will you know you are ready to live life? You will know you have arrived at your destination, Life, and that you are ready to live it when you take notice and understand the signs along the journey. Each sign will point out one of ten attributes you must have. I wish you a happy, peaceful, and fulfilling life. Live it!

Let's look at the ten attributes that allow you to live life to its fullest potential.

REFLECTION FIVE: TEN ATTRIBUTES

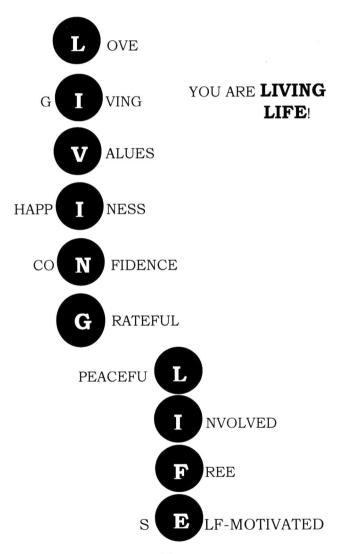

DESTINATION

Read each attribute below and highlight the ones you already embody. Take time to work on the attributes you have not highlighted.

LOVE: This is something you give, an action word. You have to have love for yourself before you can give it to someone else. It is a gift. You give it expecting nothing in return.

GIVING: If you hold on to everything and never give, you cannot receive. Keep an open heart, an open mind, and an open hand; then, extend it.

VALUES: If you do not stand for something, you will fall for anything. Always be in pursuit of peace and happiness. Do not compromise your beliefs for anyone or anything.

HAPPINESS: When you tap into your Source, you will realize you have everything you need. Circumstances will not dictate your life. You will be in charge. You will order your day and tell your ministering angels to get up and get busy because today is the best day of the rest of your life!

CONFIDENCE: Believe in yourself. Discover what your purpose is. Think about what you are passionate about, and pursue it like your life depends on it, because it does!

GRATEFUL: There is no time for pity parties. Count your blessings daily, when you awake and before you go to sleep. God don't make no junk. You are made in His image. Meditate on all He went through in order for you to have life. Live every day to show Him how grateful you are. Make God smile!

PEACEFUL: Avoid conflict and confusion. Stand still in the midst of a storm. Pray for those who do not know God. Shine your light so others may see.

INVOLVED: Be the change you want to see in the world. Start in your community. Get involved. Whatever job, organization, or committee you are in, do not just be in it. Get it in you: Be active. What can you do to make the organization better?

FREE: Financial freedom will allow you to live life abundantly. You must have a Plan B. A job is to maintain; a Plan B allows you to live life to its fullest. Do not just exist—live! Get in control of your finances and save. If you lost your job tomorrow, how long would your finances last?

SELF-MOTIVATED: Don't sweat the small stuff. Stay positive. Be a risk taker, and think outside the box. Be productive and always stay humble, willing to learn. Participate fully in life.

References

[1] Reinhold Niebuhr, "Reinhold Niebuhr Quotes," Brainy Quote, http://www.brainyquote.com/quotes/quotes/r/reinholdni100884.html.

[2] Jerry Clark, "Get Off the Nail," Finsecurity.com/homepage/quotes/mm0101.html.

[3] Andrew Ong, "The Starfish Story: You Can Make a Difference," Andrew: Inside and Insights, andrew-ong.com/2008/02/06/the-starfish-story-you-can-make-a-difference.

[4] "The Drowning Man," Truth Book, http://www.truthbook.com/stories/dsp_viewstory.cfm?storyID=489.

ABOUT THE AUTHOR

Sheilah Gill was born in Washington, DC, and she is the proud mother of one son, Roderick. She is a former teacher of 19 years and currently the CEO/President of W.E. C.A.R.E. Services, Inc. After working part-time with a retirement company, she realized many educators were dedicated to preparing youth for their futures, but no one was preparing the educators for their financial futures. In March 2003, Gill expanded her vision and resigned from teaching. Today, she and her associates continue to impact thousands of lives by teaching retirement workshops in local schools. Through her company, Gill is destined to make a difference. Having earned the prestigious six-figure income earner ring through her entrepreneurship, she is dedicated to teaching others to do the same. Gill loves people and understands that if she helps enough people get what they want, she will automatically get what she wants!

Made in the USA
Lexington, KY
10 April 2018